10 to 17
poems

10 to 17

Poems

10 to 17

Published in print and digital e-book by Little Tree Press

ISBN: 979-8-9913851-0-7

Library of Congress Control Number: 2024917957

To those who have yet to find
their place in the world.

— KC

Contents

10 to 17

Introduction

When a person is deeply consumed by their troubles and feels as though their pain will never subside, a common phrase of reassurance is provided: "time heals all wounds." We act as though time itself is the remedy to our worries. Sure, maybe time aids the healing. Or maybe, just maybe, the ability to heal from previous struggles was always within us. As time goes on, we commit ourselves to new endeavors, and pull ourselves out of the dark place we were once stuck in. It is debatable whether or not time is the catalyst for our healing, but if one thing is for certain, it's that time moves. The more time moves, the more we learn to cherish the memories we never even thought would matter, like the memories that we wanted to forget at one point but now realize are critical to the people we are today.

Or at least that was my experience. This anthology is a collection of pieces I wrote in real time at different phases of my life. You'll see various styles of writing employed that reflect whatever I was feeling, themes like innocence recurrent throughout, and how my outlook on life has changed as I have grown. These pieces are far from perfect, but I felt that I owed it to myself to honor the authenticity of how my writing/perspective evolved just like I did (so bear with the childhood enthusiasm and teenage angst, I promise it gets better).

—KC

10 to 11

A period when I pinpointed the optimism in everything. Growing up, the strength within myself, adapting, and overcoming fear. I wrote of wings, rose petals, and a bright future. I carried my poetry book wherever I went, in hand and in heart. I tried to emulate Emily Dickinson and Alfred Tennyson as I wrote about anything and everything.

"The great thing about being young and dumb is that you don't know what you can't do." — Peter Heller

The Little Girl

I'll always be a little girl
No matter young or old
I'll always hug my parents
And my identity won't be sold.

Oh the same personality
my spirit will always hold
Because every delicate memory
is a precious piece of gold.

When you're young, you see the good.
And I'm not ready
to forget my childhood.

The Rose Within My Spirit

The rose within my spirit
blossoms, blooms, and grows
For my mind knows not why
Only the angel in my heart knows.

When the petals fall from the rose
I reflect on the choices that I chose
When the petals die
I begin to doubt and cry.

When a petal disappears, all my cheers turn into fears.
And when I recover, I rise!
I shout in glee and look at the doubters
who doubted me!
Who fill my heart with sadness!

The petals of my rose grow once more, and I finally let
my spirit soar!
The angel in my heart
has helped me learn a lot.

When the petals fall
I can look at the positive
And feel all I've got.

Change

Change is the part of me left behind
A part I search to find
Fantasy lands turn into the reality of life
And future awaits like an emerald or a knife

What will change think of me?
Will it welcome me with tea?
Or will it uproar the sea?
Or will it shake the tree?

Change hovers around me like a dove
either falling or flying.
I suddenly remember the things I love, and I'm scared
that they'll be dying.
Of course I hear the angels replying
And that is why I must keep trying.
I must try to adjust to something new
So I won't feel the phases of deep, dark blue.

Trophies

Victory is glory and with glory comes pride

But with the reward, you never know

where mysteries hide.

Beneath the gold and beyond the most

Are trophies there to influence boast?

The eyes of the winner get fooled by the trick

A loser or a winner

Which one would you pick?

Satisfaction or growth?

Satisfaction is joy

And with joy comes a smile

Growth is an opportunity to learn for a while

Go on...choose

Win or lose?

A trophy can be good from a view

A trophy can discourage others, too

But deep inside that beautiful fame

Comes a little shame for others

But others should be proud

They have accomplished more than they'll ever know

The Earth

Hills and land

Flowing streams

Diversity

Hearts finding dreams

Magnificent minds

Friendship true

Justice on earth

Clear waters blue

Crystals and rubies

Wept thick tears

Learning experiences

Demon sneers

Harmonious sounds of laughter

Pats on the back

Looking at families

In a pack

Having time

Doing what you adore

A child's birth

Rose petals and smiles

This is the earth

Fear

There's nothing more shocking than fear;
no, there's not
Because fear is nothing, nothing you thought
In your sleep, it will leap, and snatch you by the ear!
And when you wake, you'll start to shake and
whimper,
"There's nothing worse than fear!"
For when you cry, it will try and eat you in a bite!
And then you'll shout, "You gave me such a fright!"

But it's okay
because you're strong.
So be daring
and prove fear wrong.

Smithereens of a Girl

Crisp, angelic, and fragile
smithereens of memories
are made of crystals and a pearl.

They all seem to represent
an adorable little girl.

Rose petals, golden harps
and red apples fresh grown
are all bold things that represent
my past well-known.

Majestic sunsets,
a voice that echoes with grace

these are the good times
I once did embrace.

Swans in my past swirled!
Angels were present in my young world!
Troubles sank below my knees!
Oh, the vision a young girl sees!

Until my emotions grew strong, and they started to hurl.

I was rising in age with wings, yet still a little girl.

12 to 14

A period where poetry evolved into songwriting. I didn't confide in writing as much as I used to. But when I did, some of my optimism began to be challenged by cynicism. I wasn't the same ten year old strutting around in French berets and declaring my life ambitions. Still, I wrote of beauty standards, and I rectified the challenges I faced by reminding myself that everything happens for a reason (even if it didn't always feel like it).

"Don't let insecurity ruin the beauty you were born with."
— Anonymous

A Starlet's Reality

Innocent girl
in the lavender dress
Sequins that line
plummeting innocence

Didn't know when
life would strike her pure heart
Change forever—
Cruelty it would impart

Hopeless romance
dwelled inside her head,
if only she could...
be someone else instead

What would she know
about struggles of life?
She's just a girl
Truth envelops her light

Did what was told
despite a drama sheath
Life takes a toll;
revealed what's underneath

Who protects her?
From the veil that conceals
the world's ego
Rotten core; the skin peels

Not an object
to give you attention
There's sudden rain
she still learns to drench in

Naive starlet.
You followed the wrong path?
Caught in shackles—
The real world, it's a trap

Beauty Standards

There's such a range of people on this earth
Beauty within everyone
but there are always standards determining worth

What is beauty really
when it's often defined?
My insecurities of appearance
sometimes linger in my mind

We live in a world of so much bad and good
Wanting to be accepted but often misunderstood
All the labels that are placed
Sometimes I feel my genuine self start to erase
Beauty standards are so high
Beauty standards are all just a lie

There are so many flaws I think I need to conceal
All these people think they can tell me how to feel

What is perfection really
when it's often expected?
All these selfless people
are still never respected

We live in a world of so much bad and good
Wanting to be accepted but often misunderstood
All the labels that are placed
Sometimes I feel my genuine self start to erase
Beauty standards are so high
Beauty standards are all just a lie

These standards
confine me in a space
All the mirrors
surrounding my face

Judgment
in every direction

All this controversy
over my reflection

Beauty standards are so high
Beauty standards are all just a lie

Everything Happens for a Reason

Dreamer girl
The optimist
Heart to the world, no, don't tighten my fist
Even when it feels like glimmers of hope start to fade
I tell myself I'll find my truth someday

Fall, winter, spring and summer
Another school year is gone but I'll still remember
That there's no me
or happily ever after
If we aren't together

Everything happens for a reason
Even through every endless season
Through the tears and the sunshine and all the
heartbreak
I float with every risk that I'm willing to take
'Cause everything happens for a reason
Though dark sometimes, this is the world
that I believe in

I'm shaped by love
And led by light
And when monsters creep in, I've learned how to fight
Even when it's too much to handle
I refuse to let someone blow out my candle

Fall, winter, spring and summer
Another school year is gone but I'll still remember
That there's no me
or happily ever after
If we aren't together

Everything happens for a reason
Even through every endless season
Through the tears and the sunshine and all the
heartbreak
I float with every risk that I'm willing to take
'Cause everything happens for a reason
Though dark sometimes, this is the world
that I believe in

Oh even when not accepted
The burnout, the slap of rejection
Life is never what you expected it to be
Don't be the one to neglect it
Somehow redirect it
Even when it affected your self esteem
'Cause I have dreams
And you have dreams, too
The scope of possibilities
You never knew

'Cause everything happens for a reason
Though dark sometimes
this is the world that I believe in

15 to 16

I found a confidante in writing prose poetry again. Yet I wasn't overflowing with love when I confided in it, I was projecting self-doubt in an environment that reaffirmed it. Glimpses of light peaked through my uncertainty, but it was often overshadowed by other turmoil out of my control. A lot of my writing consisted of streams of consciousness as I attempted to process negative thoughts.

"When a flower doesn't bloom, you fix the environment in which it grows, not the flower." — Alexander den Heijer

A Girl

A girl
who cares
too much about those who care too little.

A girl
who is sensitive
to heartless criticism.

A girl
who writes
her prowess away in a journal
as her peers perform lengthy speeches
compiled of words to simply
fill the time.

A girl
whose hair
conceals her identity
so she's yet to be understood.

A girl
who wears
earbuds to block out the noise
that seeps into her sense of self.

A girl
who listens
to music that reinforces a somewhat perpetual feeling
of her lack of understanding with the world.

A girl
who everyone thinks
is perceptive
until she accidentally unleashes
an ignorant thought
which spurs a permanent label.

A girl
who pretends
to have it figured out
to mask her naiveté.

A girl
who is scared
to let go of her innocence.

A girl
who is defined
by her innocence.

A girl
who takes
definitions to heart.

A girl
who takes
her time
but can't bear the time
she spends waiting.

A girl
whose time
was taken from her.

A girl
who wants
to recover this time wasted
and shape it into something beautiful.

A girl
who wants
to manage her time
but the time runs away
from her
until
she's out of breath.

A girl
who treasures
every breath
but it's taken away from her
when she's in awe
or on the verge of a panic attack.

The girl may treasure her life but she doesn't feel
treasured herself. She's just "a girl" that tells herself she
is insignificant. She longs for a name, but for all anyone
knows, she's just a girl who can't change who she or the
world is.

Not Really a Hero

I know the truth
behind the hero's costume
it leaves me confused
that I'm not believed but I'm bruised.

The User

I believed you

Just like I believed most promises made to me.

Because I didn't see people as threats,

I saw them as safety

I saw a relationship as a force

that could shield me from danger

But if you were the dress, then I was your hanger

I was the computer, multifaceted in its calculations yet

you were the user

Because you used me.

Broken Letters Rant

My life seems to be compiled by a lot of unanswered
questions lately.
A lot of unfinished sentences, what ifs, basking in
meaningless letters
that need proper punctuation.
My life needs someone
to just take the scramble of letters
and make sense of them.
To arrange them in coherent words
and to guide the words to find sentences.
The letters are a lost mess
that just need to know what comes next.
The letters want to become words
but they don't know how to because they think too
much about becoming extensive essays before
becoming simple words first. Maybe the letters are lost
on the page because they are not willing to accept that
they must mold into a rough draft before they can
morph into a masterpiece. The letters are broken
because they are isolated, but the cycle prolongs
because they have not found other letters that complete
them accordingly to form the right words. The letters

have a certain level of pride that holds them back because they would rather form extravagant diction than be forced into creating the shameful slang that surrounds them. The letters just need someone to believe that they can be arranged into thought-provoking sentiments. They need someone to recognize that they have what it takes to captivate readers with enough persistence, and they need a sprinkle of wisdom to be imparted upon them. Or else the letters fear they will be mistaken as an unfinished idea worth deleting, and then they may even cease from existence.

Please let a brilliant reader and writer make their way into my life, to mend the broken letters.

Tunnel Vision

Tunnel vision
Fueled by my ambition
Seeking the light at the end of the tunnel

What a world we live in
Where we rarely listen
To the unraveling of others struggles

Here I am
just clinging on to things
that I can't control

Why do I spend my time comparing myself when I
could be nurturing my soul?

I was ahead
but now I'm lost
in the pack

I'm consumed
by everything
I lack

The World Continues

The unforgiving shore meets my feet
The salt sprinkles the sugar
The wind hugs my waist
The world continues as my world subsides

Dirt spoils white shoes
The snowstorms prevail at unexpected times
My cries for an answer dissipate into shallow air
I hardly breathe this shallow air
Yet the world continues as my world subsides

My rugged hands are enlaced with dying fabric
The fabric that once held my hair up
Now my hair rests unruly
And the desert dries the gleaming strands
And so the world continues as my world subsides

The sand makes sandpaper out of my skin
And the rose thorns make roses out of my face
And the rashes burn with wrath at my mistakes
And so the world continues, as my world subsides.

To feel and think in our generation

"You're too hard on yourself" they would always tell me.
But I don't think I am.
Because in a society that expects everything from us,
I feel like I offer nothing.
In fact, I find myself becoming a burden on the
shoulders of others,
Someone who is a shame in the name of association in a
world rooted in connection.
Born in a generation infatuated with superficiality when
all I long for is to have a meaningful conversation.
But the only conversations I have are internally when I
overthink.
"Overthinking is the thief of happiness," people say.
And they're right. But people also say a lot of things
they don't mean.
People make promises that they can't keep.
Then trust is broken, and wounds are engraved in
former compassion.
Those who have their most beloved hopes and dreams
shattered into smithereens are the ones that grow into
people misunderstood.

We feel like we're not in control.
We long for the control.

We think and feel that we have to aspire to something
great, that we have to make a name for ourselves,
something to be proud of to feel and think we're valid.
We can feel trapped in our own minds,
try to defy societal norms,
but at the end of the day, we all care at least a little what
other people think.
So we feel disgraced with ourselves.
And we overthink.
And we do both until we feel incapable of doing
anything anymore.
I once was that sunshine,
until I felt the need to hide away.

People can make assumptions about whatever they
want to, people can say what they want to say, but it is
so rare that someone truly seeks the truth.
Our generation cares about our appearances more than
what lies underneath.
And so I fear.

I fear that nobody wants to get to truly know me.
To know my truth.
So I fail to connect sometimes because I feel and think
that I am a burden.

I'm too hard on myself, people have told me. Then why
am I always made to feel and think I'm inadequate? Is it
me, is it you, or is it all of us? That's the real question.

Memory Garden

We laugh in our bruised garden
The one we made as kids
The kind you could get lost in
back in our innocence

Now the weeds wrap our ankles
And our footprints glue our stance
we wanted to visit memories
So guess now was our chance

We absorbed our perspiration
And the dirt beneath our toes
The house we would soon be leaving
And the sunflower where it grows

Oh.

The garden will no longer be our home.

Goodbye to all we've ever known.

And we'll be on our own.

goodbye to this little town
where I was never found

Like a Dandelion

Even in the midst of the floods that have drenched my grounds, the grip that has taken hold of me, stripping me of air when intrusive thoughts seem to clench the inner workings of my mind, or the seesaw within me that swings between defeated and empty, there are moments where life's beauty taps me on the shoulder and so I turn around. Just a gentle tap. A loving tap. And I realize that there are moments of realization in life, and these moments are dispersed and gratify the people who need them like feathery bristles of dandelions dispersing after a wish is made. These moments strike me every so often and I freeze in time, absorbing the simplicity that leaves me content somehow.

17

A note to younger me —

Don't take it so personally.

A comment you hear is not a reflection of you, my sweet girl. It was never you. That one judgment, snide comment, or glare in your direction is not indicative of your value. You are so much more. Understand that everyone has different experiences, is in different phases of their life, and has different world views in some capacity.

You don't have to please everyone.

"Happiness is letting go of what you think your life is supposed to look like." — Mandy Hale

Sunlight

Finally,
I opened the blinds
allowing sunlight to drip into the room.
I let it fill my heart and my conscience, and I honed in
the gleam of iridescent closure.
The glare didn't feel too overwhelming this time,
astonishing me that after months in the shadows that
my eyes could soak up such a blazing sight.
But there it was, greeting me
as I always anticipated it would.
A threshold into a new chapter
One I knew was destined to find me
That I could meet halfway.

Poetry

The words that have always seemed to flutter in my
subconscious going unsaid.
I miss the way the wings flapped,
knowing what was ahead.
The intellect that reverberated in every piece of mind.
The pieces morphed, like the creature, with time.
Who knew that poetry in me might fade?
I forget its weight, the fears it assuaged.
I forgot what it meant when other things found
meaning.
Yet I know it's a home that I'll never truly be leaving.

I'll return when disorder lines like dominos.
In a nonsensical world, poetry sometimes feels like
all I really know.

*Just because life gets fifty percent better doesn't mean
you'll feel a hundred percent complete right away.*

Castle Hill

A misty dew clenches the air

The tide pulls and releases, tensing its muscles with
breaths of persistence

Rippling and rippling, tickling my feet with brush
strokes of gelid water

It has yet to amass the rock

Or myself completely

It showers the sand with affection

This is the kind of place

I would run away to in my dreams

Secluded from troubles

In the midst of harmonious waters and cooling fog

Standing on the precipice

Of God knows what.

Detached from treacherous times

That crave to claw me into formidable unknowns

Yet my stance cements me here

In this moment

Making me a distant observer of tumultuous realities

I'm safe.

Or so I thought.

Suddenly, the water arrogates a melancholy persona
Suddenly, the fog fumes with fury
Suddenly, the rock that once steadied me seizes me
Suddenly, the place I begged to run away to became the
place I wanted to run away from.

A Fable of a Person

I believe the words you utter, like symphonies of
promise
I listen to grandiose tales, you tell of pacifying
battles
I laugh at your witty remarks, that were never even
funny
I dismiss your inner demons, convincing myself that I'm
crazy
I look you in the eye, offering my indebted
gratitude
I deem you my mentor, knowing little about the word's
etymology
I fall into all your mouse traps, hidden in plain
sight
I bled finally from all your poison, slowly quelling
who I used to be
I decimate your dishes of deception into shards,
your lies no longer tolerable
I escape the false world you meticulously painted
I bury boxes of remembrance in my closet's
abyss

And yet after you ravaged my normalcy into ruins
I crave validation from versions of you
illustrated in other fonts

Broken

Many people are broken.

Sometimes it's a subtle dent you didn't even notice at first glance on your car, other times it's as if life ripped them apart like a merciless child did with their least favorite teddy bear.

Regardless, everyone has some hurt in them.

As you smile, ready to share your personal win with others, it may coincide with the moment a person loses their job.

Or experienced the death of a loved one.

Or maybe an internal battle roils inside them that has lingered for a while.

Don't make the mistake of assuming a smile is a signal of immunity.

Or that one's aptitude or beauty automatically equates to happiness.

You never really know with people.

And they never really know what's truly going on with you, do they?

Perfectionism

is the voice in your head

gnawing away at the rope

tying your thoughts together

with your self compassion.

Hindering any sense of abundance,

Clinging to a craving

of jumping higher

running faster

chasing an infinite finish line.

It seems too infinite

for the current version of you to handle.

The voice is augmented

and continues to scathe the rope

please keep the rope intact

don't let it go

don't let the daunting voice tug at loose ends of your

sense of self

Not impossible

Whenever things frustrated me
Like negative implications infused into backhanded
compliments or condescending comments
My mom told me "just let it roll off your back!"
It's not that easy, I would say.
Whenever I scrutinized blemishes on my skin
Or the way a dress either hugged me
or sagged against my skin
My mom would say
"you must have more confidence in yourself!"
It's not that easy, I would say.
I convinced myself that irritable acts were irrevocable
and that confidence was unattainable.
I didn't know how I could just feel unbothered
or certain.
Now I do.
But there's no quick antidote, no shortcut, no words
that will give you those traits if you are unwilling to
accept them.
"It's not that easy"
but it doesn't make it impossible.

Somewhere between then and now, your spirit healed.

The Test of Time

Isn't it strange
how a person that once made your heart swell
Someone who beckoned you into their life
A person whose world you immersed yourself in
like it was your own
can disappear from your life
when you thought
you needed them the most.

Your every thought once attached to their being
Pleading for their approval
Yet none of it
matters
anymore.

Isn't it strange
how suddenly
It feels like a lifetime ago.
You finally muster the courage to look at them on an
ordinary Tuesday afternoon when your paths cross

The test of time looks you in the eye
This time, you realize that forces no longer push you
together.

You no longer hear their name everywhere you go.
You no longer see iterations of the same car they drove
in parking lots

You no longer conjure scenarios out of thin air where
they engender joy
no one else could give you.
You no longer care.

In an odd way, you know the universe is creating a
barrier.
All for your own good.
This was how it was supposed to be.

The Gift You Can Give Yourself

A misconception about happiness
is that it's a lucky package
that arrives at your doorstep on a fateful day.
It's believed that as time passes
a person will send you that package
and gift you your happiness.

But under that belief,
doesn't that mean your happiness is in the hands of
others?
The truth is that you can choose happiness.
But the vices in your mind
are often holding you back
without you realizing it.

It is believed that happiness will grace people
in rare happenstances.
But you have the power
to create a golden light for yourself
that will forge paths
greater than you could have ever possibly imagined.

You've convinced yourself for so long
that you must comply to the behavior of automatons all
around you
scrolling, judging, and comparing on social media.
So you scrolled, and scrolled, seeking gratification
a device could never give you.
But you can choose a new path for yourself.

Don't lock yourself in your room waiting for the
package to arrive.
Go out and craft your own version.
Craft your own happiness.

Somehow

I love the word somehow.

Somehow, I'm here, existing.

Somehow, I'm happy despite the circumstances.

Somehow, my life has changed in every way imaginable.

Yet I made it, somehow.

Continuing to thrive, somehow.

It all turned out okay, somehow.

Somehow, defying the odds.

And I'm better because of the "somehows."

Alive (an ode to self-expression)

They call you a dying art
One not worth salvaging
But I see beauty tucked in all your strands
Stored away in bookshelves
Dust coating your worn out spine
Let me trace the dust with polished fingerprints
Grasp the words you crave to be read in the palms of
careful hands
Let me illuminate your dull hues of black and white text
With reimagined thoughts of the present
You are not obsolete
You are not washed up on abandoned shores
Your prevalence will be perennial
As long as I have a say

Like My Favorite Book

I love you like my favorite book.

Yes, I admit your cover was what drew me in.

Looking at you, I saw vibrant colors and intricate art too

irresistible to simply pass.

But as you opened up for me to read,

your content and character far surpassed

the allure that initially enticed me.

Your words resound with wisdom, and even though I

want to take all of them in, absorb them like a sponge

does with water in one sitting, I know I must be patient.

Pages of your life story, an equilibrium of dire and

tranquil waters, could never bore me even after the

thousandth page.

Unlike my favorite book, you're an ever-evolving story

that has yet to be finished.

There is not a decisive ending to you.

There are pages to be added that I get to write.

That we get to write together.

I Love You, Grandma

Grandma,

I love your aroma of daffodils diffused in tender hugs

I love how you hold us with a fierce grasp emanating pure love and strength

I love when you speak of verdant foliage, peering through your window, smiling just for you

I love when you offer peach slices, percolating with a sugary dew only you can bring to fruition

I love watching you give life to a heap of vegetables and dough and transform it into twigim

I love that your love language is food, and how you take joy in our nourishment

I love how your eyes twinkle when we share our pieces of good news

I love how you thoughtfully save your gold pineapple necklace and charm bracelet for special occasions

I love how you stand outside waving to us, to ensure a proper goodbye

I love playing assortments of board games with you, being blessed by unexpected fortunes

I love how you choose to see the best,

both in uncharted waters and the ones you love

There are so many things to love about you, Grandma.

And I love that you have so much love to give.

Still, You Can

Still, you can drive aimlessly on interminable roads
blasting blaring music
Still, you can meander around the mall, mulling over
makeup's price
Still, you can ensconce yourself in blankets, binging
basic rom coms
Still, you can peer patiently through your window,
waiting for your friends' arrivals
Still, you can let laughter lead your light, or let your
light lead all your laughter
Still, you can romanticize mundane work, wishing it
was wonderful
Still, you can indulge in sweets, savoring cupcake
sprinkles
Still, you can scream at concerts, your concerns no
longer visible
Still, you can find your soulmate, starry eyed the day
they see you
Still you can play that character, to a degree your family
won't believe it's you
Still you can do all the things
you always dreamed to do
Time hasn't quite outrun you yet, so embrace where life
leads you to

Dear Self a Year From Now

I must admit I envy the knowledge you possess.
You have the luxury of knowing how a gargantuan
milestone unravels
as you pack your bags on the way to college
While my current self grapples with tethering disparate
threads
as I synthesize who I am in a 650 word statement.
Are you happy?
Don't show me contrived pictures of yourself smiling on
social media
to prove to me that you are
I want to know, are you authentically, unequivocally
happy?

Because I'm not.
At least not at the moment I write this.
I have devoted myself wholeheartedly to you
Bore burdens so you wouldn't have to
I've sacrificed my life for a life
I hypothetically could live
All in the name of your future reputation.

I know that vestiges of my current identity will reside
in you
As others fall away

And I know that unprecedented variables will enter
your life
Beyond just the ones you are forced to isolate in math
class

Even so

I hope impostor syndrome doesn't dishevel you
I hope pernicious perfectionism isn't bequeathed to you
I hope the malice that others inflict doesn't curtail your
strides of progress
And I hope your values adhere to your core even as the
world rotates around your axis of familiarity

I'm sorry if I've failed you
And you know better than anyone that
A fear of failing has been ingrained in me
Since the day I took my first breath

But I want you to know that I'm proud of you even if I'm
a bit envious
Are you proud of yourself?
I'm sure you have learned from my mistakes and know
now not to repeat them
I'm sure you'll remember me and will speak fondly of
me when you share anecdotes with your friends,
laughing about your past naïveté

And I'm sure a steady head rests on your shoulders, as
you set out to embark on your life's trajectory

I don't tell you this enough, but I love you, and I can't
wait to meet the person you've become.

About the Author

Kate Clemetson is a poet, singer, and songwriter who loves creating original works that capture her authentic experiences. Since age ten, she has taken joy in writing poetry and began writing her own songs at the age of twelve. Originally from the San Francisco Bay Area, she now resides in New Jersey, though wherever she goes, she takes her passion for the arts with her.

www.ingramcontent.com/pod-product-compliance
Lightning Source LLC
Chambersburg PA
CBHW031004090426
42737CB00008B/669